Table Of Contents

The Path to True Love: A Guide to Finding Your Soul Mate

Chapter 1: Understanding the Concept of Soul Mates

Defining Soul Mates

The concept of soul mates has been romanticized in movies and literature, but what exactly does it mean to find your soul mate? A soul mate is often described as a person who is uniquely suited to you in every way, someone who understands you on a deeper level than anyone else. They are your perfect match, your other half, the missing piece to your puzzle.

But finding your soul mate is not just about finding someone who complements you perfectly. It is also about finding someone who challenges you to grow and evolve, someone who supports you in becoming the best version of yourself. Your soul mate is someone who sees your flaws and imperfections and loves you unconditionally anyway.

Soul mates can come into our lives in many different ways. Whether through online dating, mutual interests and hobbies, spiritual connections, or even after a divorce or breakup, the key is to remain open and receptive to the possibility of finding your soul mate. As a single parent, in a long-distance relationship, in a same-sex relationship, or in a multicultural or interfaith relationship, there are unique challenges that may arise, but true love knows no boundaries.

No matter where you are in life, whether you are experiencing heartbreak or embarking on a journey of self-discovery and personal growth, your soul mate is out there waiting for you. Keep an open heart and mind, trust in the universe, and believe that true love will find its way to you when the time is right.

The Importance of Finding Your Soul Mate

Finding your soul mate is a journey that many people embark on in their lifetime. Whether you are looking for love after a divorce, as a single parent, in a long-distance relationship, or later in life, the importance of finding your soul mate cannot be understated. In my book, "The Path to True Love: A Guide to Finding Your Soul Mate," I explore the various ways in which you can find your soul mate and the significance of this connection in your life.

One of the key aspects of finding your soul mate is through self-discovery and personal growth. By understanding yourself and what you truly desire in a partner, you can attract the right person into your life. This involves taking the time to reflect on your values, beliefs, and goals, and being open to learning more about yourself along the way.

For those who are using online dating to find their soul mate, it is important to approach the process with an open heart and mind. Be honest in your profile and communicate your desires clearly to potential matches. Finding your soul mate through mutual interests and hobbies can also be a powerful way to connect with someone who shares your passions and values.

In addition, finding your soul mate through spiritual connections and compatibility can bring a deeper level of understanding and connection to your relationship. Whether you are in a same-sex relationship, a multicultural or interfaith relationship, or have experienced heartbreak in the past, there is always hope for finding your soul mate.

Ultimately, finding your soul mate is about being true to yourself and being open to the possibilities that the universe has in store for you. By following the guidance in my book, you can take the necessary steps to attract your soul mate and experience true love in your life.

Myths and Misconceptions about Soul Mates

In the world of love and relationships, the concept of soul mates holds a special place in many people's hearts. However, there are several myths and misconceptions surrounding the idea of finding your soul mate that can lead to confusion and frustration in the search for true love.

One common myth about soul mates is that there is only one perfect person out there for each of us. This belief can create unrealistic expectations and put pressure on individuals to find that one elusive soul mate. In reality, there are many potential soul mates out there, and finding the right person is more about compatibility and connection than some predetermined destiny.

Another misconception is that soul mates are always meant to be together, no matter what. While soul mates can have a deep and lasting connection, relationships still require effort, communication, and compromise to thrive. It's important to remember that even soul mates may face challenges and obstacles along the way.

Some people also believe that soul mates will magically appear in their lives without any effort on their part. While fate may play a role in bringing soul mates together, actively seeking out opportunities to meet new people and build meaningful connections is essential in finding true love.

By dispelling these myths and misconceptions about soul mates, individuals can approach their search for true love with a more realistic and open-minded perspective. Whether you are navigating the world of online dating, exploring mutual interests and hobbies, or seeking spiritual connections and compatibility, keeping an open heart and mind can lead you to your soul mate in unexpected and beautiful ways. Remember, true love knows no boundaries and can be found in any circumstance or stage of life.

Chapter 2: How to Find Your Soul Mate
Setting Intentions and Manifesting Your Ideal Partner

Setting intentions and manifesting your ideal partner is a powerful practice that can help you attract the love you truly desire. Whether you are looking for your soul mate through online dating, mutual interests and hobbies, spiritual connections, or after a divorce or breakup, setting intentions can help guide you on your path to true love.

To begin, take some time to reflect on what qualities you are looking for in a partner. What values are important to you? What characteristics do you admire in others? Once you have a clear vision of what you want in a relationship, write it down as if it has already happened. For example, you could say, "I am in a loving, supportive relationship with my soul mate who shares my passion for travel and adventure."

Next, visualize yourself in this relationship. Imagine how it feels to be with your ideal partner, how they make you feel loved and cherished. Allow yourself to feel the emotions that come with being in this loving relationship. This will help you align your energy with what you are trying to manifest.

Finally, trust in the universe to bring your ideal partner into your life. Be open to opportunities that come your way and take inspired action towards finding love. Remember that finding your soul mate is not about searching for them, but rather about allowing them to come into your life when the time is right.

No matter what your circumstances may be - whether you are a single parent, in a long-distance relationship, or looking for love later in life - setting intentions and manifesting your ideal partner can help you attract the love you deserve. Trust in the process and believe that true love is possible for you.

Identifying Your Relationship Needs and Deal Breakers

Before embarking on the journey to finding your soul mate, it is crucial to take the time to identify your relationship needs and deal breakers. Understanding what you truly desire in a partner and what you cannot compromise on will help you navigate the dating world with clarity and confidence.

Start by reflecting on your past relationships and experiences. What qualities did your ex-partners possess that you appreciated? What behaviors or traits were deal breakers for you? By analyzing your past, you can gain insights into what you need and what you can do without in a relationship.

Next, consider your values, beliefs, and goals. What are the non-negotiables for you in a partner when it comes to shared values and life goals? Are you looking for someone who shares your spiritual beliefs or someone who is on the same page as you when it comes to starting a family?

It is also important to think about your emotional and physical needs. Are you someone who requires a lot of emotional support and affection? Do you have specific physical preferences or requirements in a partner?

By taking the time to identify your relationship needs and deal breakers, you will be better equipped to recognize when you have found your soul mate. You will be able to communicate your needs effectively and ensure that you are in a relationship that fulfills you emotionally, spiritually, and physically. Remember, it is important to stay true to yourself and your needs in order to find true love.

Cultivating Self-Love and Worthiness

Cultivating self-love and worthiness is an essential step on the path to finding your soul mate. In order to attract the love you desire and deserve, you must first love and value yourself. This involves recognizing your own worth, embracing your strengths and weaknesses, and practicing self-care and self-compassion.

One way to cultivate self-love is by engaging in regular self-care practices, such as exercise, healthy eating, meditation, and spending time doing things that bring you joy. Taking care of your physical, emotional, and spiritual well-being will not only help you feel more confident and happy, but it will also make you more attractive to potential partners.

Another important aspect of cultivating self-love is learning to set boundaries and prioritize your own needs and desires. This means saying no to things that don't serve you, speaking up for yourself, and surrounding yourself with people who support and uplift you.

Additionally, practicing self-compassion and forgiveness is crucial in developing a healthy sense of self-worth. Be kind to yourself, especially in times of struggle or failure. Remember that you are human, and it's okay to make mistakes. Treat yourself with the same love and understanding that you would offer to a dear friend.

By cultivating self-love and worthiness, you will not only enhance your own life, but you will also become more open and receptive to the love that is meant for you. Remember, true love starts from within.

Chapter 3: Finding Your Soul Mate Through Online Dating

Creating an Authentic and Compelling Online Profile

In today's digital age, creating an authentic and compelling online profile is essential when it comes to finding your soul mate. Your online presence is often the first impression potential partners will have of you, so it's important to make it a true reflection of who you are.

When crafting your online profile, be honest and transparent about your interests, values, and goals. Avoid the temptation to embellish or exaggerate, as this can lead to disappointment and confusion down the line. Instead, focus on highlighting your unique qualities and what makes you special.

Choosing the right photos is also crucial in creating an attractive online profile. Select images that are clear, recent, and show off your personality. Avoid using overly edited or misleading photos, as this can lead to unrealistic expectations and disappointment when meeting in person.

When it comes to writing your bio, be sure to showcase your personality and what you're looking for in a partner. Use language that is positive, upbeat, and inviting. Avoid negativity or listing a laundry list of requirements, as this can be off-putting to potential matches.

Lastly, don't be afraid to show your vulnerable side in your online profile. Sharing your hopes, dreams, and fears can help create a deeper connection with potential partners. Remember, authenticity is key when it comes to finding your soul mate.

By creating an authentic and compelling online profile, you'll increase your chances of attracting like-minded individuals who are truly compatible with you. So take the time to craft a profile that accurately represents who you are, and watch as the right connections start to come your way.

Navigating the Online Dating World with Confidence

Navigating the online dating world can be a daunting task, but with confidence and a positive mindset, you can increase your chances of finding your soul mate. In today's digital age, online dating has become a popular way to meet potential partners, and it can be a great tool in your journey to finding true love.

When using online dating platforms, it's important to approach the process with confidence. Believe in yourself and know that you are worthy of love. Be clear about what you are looking for in a partner and don't settle for anything less. Trust your instincts and don't be afraid to take the first step in initiating conversations with people who catch your eye.

Finding your soul mate through online dating requires patience and perseverance. It may take time to find someone who truly resonates with you, so don't get discouraged if you don't find your perfect match right away. Stay open-minded and be willing to explore different options. Remember that the right person for you is out there, and with a positive attitude and a proactive approach, you can increase your chances of finding them.

Ultimately, navigating the online dating world with confidence means staying true to yourself and your values. Be authentic in your interactions with others and don't be afraid to show your true self. By being genuine and open, you can attract the right kind of people into your life and increase your chances of finding your soul mate through the vast landscape of online dating.

Red Flags to Watch Out for in Online Dating

Online dating can be a convenient and effective way to find your soul mate, but it's important to be aware of red flags that may indicate potential problems in a relationship. Here are some red flags to watch out for in online dating:

1. Inconsistent or evasive communication: If your potential soul mate is vague about their whereabouts, job, or personal life, it could be a sign that they are not being honest with you.

2. Pressure to move too quickly: If your online match is pushing for a commitment or intimacy before you feel comfortable, it's a red flag that they may not have your best interests at heart.

3. Lack of respect or boundaries: If your match is disrespectful towards you or disregards your boundaries, it's a sign that they may not be capable of building a healthy and respectful relationship.

4. Unwillingness to meet in person: If your match is hesitant or makes excuses to avoid meeting in person, it could be a sign that they are not who they claim to be or are not serious about pursuing a relationship.

5. Inconsistent behavior: If your match's actions do not align with their words, it may indicate that they are not being genuine or are hiding something from you.

Remember to trust your instincts and prioritize your safety and well-being when navigating the world of online dating. By being aware of these red flags, you can protect yourself and increase your chances of finding a genuine and fulfilling connection with your soul mate.

Chapter 4: Finding Your Soul Mate Through Mutual Interests and Hobbies

Exploring Shared Passions and Activities

One of the most effective ways to find your soul mate is by exploring shared passions and activities. When you engage in activities that you both enjoy, you are more likely to bond and connect on a deeper level. Whether it's a love for hiking, cooking, or painting, finding common interests can lead to a strong and lasting connection.

For those who are using online dating to find their soul mate, it's important to highlight your interests and hobbies in your profile. This will attract like-minded individuals who share your passions and increase the chances of finding someone who truly understands and appreciates you.

If you prefer to find your soul mate through mutual interests and hobbies in person, consider joining clubs, classes, or groups that align with your interests. This allows you to meet new people who share your passions and may lead to finding that special someone who shares your values and beliefs.

For those seeking a soul mate through spiritual connections and compatibility, it's essential to engage in practices and activities that align with your spiritual beliefs. Whether it's meditation, yoga, or attending religious services, connecting with others who share your spiritual values can deepen your connection and lead to a meaningful relationship.

No matter your circumstances, whether you're a single parent, in a long-distance relationship, or starting over after a breakup, exploring shared passions and activities can help you find your soul mate. By focusing on what brings you joy and fulfillment, you are more likely to attract someone who complements and enhances your life in a meaningful way. So don't be afraid to embrace your interests and hobbies, as they may lead you to the love of your life.

Joining Clubs or Groups to Meet Like-Minded Individuals

Joining clubs or groups can be a fantastic way to meet like-minded individuals who share your interests and values. Whether you are looking for new friends or hoping to find your soul mate, being part of a club or group can increase your chances of meeting someone who is truly compatible with you.

If you are struggling to find your soul mate, consider joining a club or group that aligns with your passions and hobbies. This could be anything from a book club to a hiking group to a cooking class. By surrounding yourself with people who share your interests, you are more likely to meet someone who understands and appreciates the things that are important to you.

In addition to meeting potential soul mates, joining clubs or groups can also help you expand your social circle and build meaningful relationships. Even if you don't find your soul mate right away, you may make new friends who can offer support and companionship as you continue on your journey to finding true love.

Remember, finding your soul mate is not always easy, but by putting yourself out there and joining clubs or groups, you are increasing your chances of meeting someone special who truly understands and connects with you on a deeper level. So don't be afraid to step outside of your comfort zone and try something new – you never know who you might meet along the way.

Building a Strong Connection Through Common Interests

Building a strong connection through common interests is a powerful way to find your soul mate. When you share hobbies, passions, or values with someone, it creates a strong foundation for a lasting relationship. Whether you are searching for your soul mate through online dating, mutual interests and hobbies, spiritual connections, or any other avenue, finding common ground is essential.

One of the most effective ways to connect with someone on a deeper level is to engage in activities that you both enjoy. This could be anything from hiking in nature, cooking together, attending a spiritual retreat, or participating in a book club. When you bond over shared interests, it can lead to meaningful conversations, laughter, and a sense of belonging.

If you are going through a divorce or breakup, finding someone who shares your interests can be a healing experience. It can help you rediscover yourself and your passions, while also opening the door to a new and fulfilling relationship. Similarly, if you are a single parent, connecting with someone who understands and appreciates your lifestyle can be incredibly rewarding.

In a long-distance relationship, finding common interests can bridge the physical gap between you and your soul mate. It can create a sense of closeness and intimacy, even when you are miles apart. And in a same-sex relationship, multicultural or interfaith relationship, or any other unique situation, shared interests can help you navigate challenges and celebrate your differences.

No matter where you are in life or what obstacles you may be facing, building a strong connection through common interests is a powerful way to find your soul mate. By exploring your passions, values, and hobbies, you can attract someone who truly understands and appreciates you for who you are. So embrace your interests, connect with like-minded individuals, and open your heart to the possibility of finding true love.

Chapter 5: Finding Your Soul Mate Through Spiritual Connections and Compatibility

Understanding the Role of Spirituality in Relationships

Spirituality plays a crucial role in relationships, especially when it comes to finding your soul mate. When two individuals are spiritually connected and compatible, they are able to form a deeper and more meaningful bond that goes beyond the physical realm. This connection allows them to understand each other on a soul level, leading to a more fulfilling and harmonious relationship.

For those on the path to finding their soul mate, it is important to explore and understand their own spiritual beliefs and values. By doing so, they can better align themselves with potential partners who share similar beliefs and values. This spiritual connection can create a strong foundation for a lasting and loving relationship.

Finding your soul mate through spiritual connections and compatibility can also help in navigating challenges and conflicts that may arise in the relationship. When both partners are spiritually aligned, they are able to approach issues with compassion, empathy, and understanding. This allows them to work through their differences in a more constructive and loving way.

Whether you are finding your soul mate after a divorce or breakup, as a single parent, in a long-distance relationship, or in any other unique situation, spiritual compatibility can be a guiding force in your search for true love. By focusing on spiritual connections and values, you can open yourself up to a deeper and more authentic connection with your soul mate.

Seeking Out Partners with Similar Beliefs and Values

When embarking on the journey to find your soul mate, it is essential to seek out partners who share similar beliefs and values as you. This is crucial for building a strong and lasting relationship based on mutual understanding and respect.

One way to find a partner with similar beliefs and values is through online dating. Many dating websites and apps allow you to filter potential matches based on specific criteria, such as religious beliefs, political views, and lifestyle choices. By being upfront about your own beliefs and values in your online dating profile, you can attract like-minded individuals who are looking for the same things in a relationship.

Another way to connect with potential soul mates who share your beliefs and values is through mutual interests and hobbies. Joining clubs, groups, or organizations that align with your passions can help you meet people who have similar outlooks on life and relationships. Whether it's a love for hiking, cooking, or volunteering, shared interests can be a powerful foundation for a meaningful connection.

For those who place a strong emphasis on spiritual connections and compatibility, seeking out partners who share your beliefs can be a transformative experience. Whether you practice the same religion or share similar spiritual philosophies, finding someone who understands and supports your spiritual journey can deepen the bond between you and your soul mate.

No matter your background or past experiences, finding a soul mate with similar beliefs and values is possible. Whether you are navigating the world of online dating, exploring mutual interests and hobbies, or seeking spiritual connections, being open and authentic about who you are and what you value is key to attracting a partner who is truly meant for you. By seeking out partners who align with your beliefs and values, you are taking a crucial step towards finding your true love and creating a fulfilling and lasting relationship.

Enhancing Spiritual Connection with Your Soul Mate

When it comes to finding your soul mate, it is important to not only focus on physical and emotional compatibility, but also on enhancing your spiritual connection with each other. Building a strong spiritual connection can deepen your bond and create a sense of unity that transcends the physical world.

One way to enhance your spiritual connection with your soul mate is to engage in spiritual practices together. This could include meditating together, attending spiritual retreats or workshops, or simply having deep and meaningful conversations about your beliefs and values. By sharing these experiences, you can strengthen your connection on a spiritual level.

Another important aspect of enhancing your spiritual connection with your soul mate is to practice gratitude and appreciation for each other. Take the time to express your love and gratitude for your partner, and be open to receiving the same in return. By cultivating an attitude of gratitude, you can create a positive and loving energy that will nourish your spiritual connection.

It is also important to trust your intuition and listen to your inner voice when it comes to your relationship. Your intuition can guide you towards your soul mate and help you navigate any challenges that may arise. Trusting in the power of your intuition can deepen your spiritual connection with your partner and bring you closer together.

By focusing on enhancing your spiritual connection with your soul mate, you can create a relationship that is built on love, trust, and mutual respect. Remember to nurture your spiritual connection through shared practices, gratitude, and intuition, and watch as your bond with your soul mate grows stronger and deeper with each passing day.

Chapter 6: Finding Your Soul Mate After a Divorce or Breakup

Healing from Past Relationships and Opening Your Heart Again

Healing from past relationships is an essential step on the path to finding your soul mate. It can be difficult to open your heart again after experiencing heartbreak, but it is necessary in order to make room for true love to enter your life.

One of the first steps in healing from past relationships is to take the time to reflect on what went wrong and what lessons you can learn from the experience. This self-reflection can help you to identify any patterns or behaviors that may have contributed to the end of the relationship, allowing you to make positive changes moving forward.

It is also important to forgive both yourself and your ex-partner for any mistakes that were made in the relationship. Holding onto anger and resentment will only weigh you down and prevent you from moving forward in a healthy way.

Opening your heart again after a breakup or divorce can be a scary prospect, but it is necessary in order to find true love. One way to do this is to focus on self-care and self-love, taking the time to nurture yourself and build up your self-esteem.

When you are ready to start dating again, it is important to approach new relationships with an open heart and a positive attitude. Be willing to let go of the past and embrace the possibility of finding your soul mate.

By healing from past relationships and opening your heart again, you will be in a much better position to attract the kind of love and connection that you truly deserve. Trust in the process and believe that true love is out there waiting for you.

Embracing Lessons Learned from Previous Partnerships

In the journey to finding your soul mate, it is important to reflect on the lessons learned from previous partnerships. Each relationship we experience is a stepping stone towards finding true love, and it is crucial to take the time to understand what went wrong in the past in order to create a better future.

One of the key lessons to embrace from previous partnerships is communication. Many relationships falter due to a lack of open and honest communication. Take the time to reflect on how communication played a role in past relationships and strive to improve this aspect in future partnerships.

Another important lesson to learn is setting boundaries. It is essential to establish boundaries in a relationship to ensure that both partners feel respected and valued. Reflect on past relationships where boundaries were crossed and use those experiences to set clear boundaries in future partnerships.

Additionally, it is important to embrace the lesson of self-love and self-care. Oftentimes, we lose ourselves in relationships and neglect our own needs. Take the time to prioritize self-love and self-care, and remember that you deserve to be happy and fulfilled in a relationship.

By embracing the lessons learned from previous partnerships, you will be better equipped to find your soul mate. Use these experiences as a guide to creating a healthy and fulfilling relationship that is built on communication, boundaries, and self-love. Remember, each relationship is a learning experience that brings you one step closer to finding true love.

Moving Forward with Hope and Optimism

Moving forward with hope and optimism is essential when embarking on the journey to finding your soul mate. It's important to remain positive and open-minded, as love can come when you least expect it. Whether you are searching for your soul mate through online dating, mutual interests, spiritual connections, or any other means, having a hopeful outlook will attract positive energy into your life.

If you have experienced a divorce or breakup, it's natural to feel discouraged or hesitant about finding love again. However, it's crucial to remember that every ending is a new beginning. Use your past experiences as lessons to grow and evolve, and trust that the right person will come into your life when the time is right.

As a single parent, it can be challenging to balance the responsibilities of raising children while also seeking a romantic partner. Remember that finding your soul mate is possible, and being a parent can actually enhance the connection you have with someone who understands and appreciates your family dynamic.

Whether you are in a long-distance relationship, same-sex relationship, multicultural or interfaith relationship, or are searching for love later in life, maintaining hope and optimism is key. Every individual is deserving of true love, and by focusing on personal growth and self-discovery, you will attract a partner who aligns with your values and beliefs.

No matter what obstacles or challenges you may face in your quest for love, moving forward with hope and optimism will guide you towards finding your soul mate. Trust in the universe's plan for you, and remain open to the endless possibilities that await on your path to true love.

Chapter 7: Finding Your Soul Mate as a Single Parent

Balancing Parenting Responsibilities with Dating

Balancing parenting responsibilities with dating can be a challenging task, but it is possible to find your soul mate while still being a dedicated parent. As a single parent, your children are your top priority, but it is important to remember that you deserve love and companionship as well.

One key aspect of balancing parenting responsibilities with dating is time management. It is essential to find a balance between spending quality time with your children and making time for your own personal life. This may mean scheduling date nights when your children are with a babysitter or arranging playdates for them while you go out on a date.

Communication is also crucial when it comes to dating as a single parent. Be open and honest with your potential partner about your responsibilities as a parent and make sure they are understanding and supportive of your situation. Finding someone who is willing to embrace your role as a parent can make the dating process much smoother.

Additionally, involving your children in the process of finding your soul mate can be beneficial. Introducing them to your potential partner early on can help them feel comfortable and secure with the idea of you dating. It is important to take things slow and not rush into blending families until you are sure it is the right decision for everyone involved.

Overall, balancing parenting responsibilities with dating requires patience, understanding, and compromise. By prioritizing your children while also making time for your own happiness, you can successfully find your soul mate while navigating the challenges of single parenthood.

Introducing Your Children to a New Partner

When you have found your soul mate and you are ready to take the next step in your relationship, it is important to consider how to introduce your children to your new partner. This can be a delicate situation, especially if your children are still processing the changes from a divorce or breakup. Here are some tips to help make the introduction a smooth and positive experience for everyone involved.

First and foremost, be open and honest with your children about your new relationship. Let them know that you have met someone special and that you care about them deeply. Reassure them that your love for them will not change and that they will always be a priority in your life.

It is also important to take things slow when introducing your children to your new partner. Start by including them in casual activities, such as going out for ice cream or playing a game in the park. This will allow them to get to know your partner in a low-pressure environment.

When the time comes to have a more formal introduction, be sure to talk to your children beforehand about what to expect. Reassure them that it is normal to feel nervous or uncertain, but that you believe they will get along well with your partner.

Above all, be patient and understanding throughout the process. Your children may need time to adjust to the idea of your new partner, and it is important to respect their feelings and give them the space they need to come to terms with the changes in their lives.

By approaching the introduction of your children to your new partner with sensitivity and care, you can help to create a strong foundation for a happy and harmonious blended family.

Nurturing a Healthy Relationship as a Blended Family

Navigating the complexities of a blended family can be challenging, but with love, patience, and understanding, it is possible to create a harmonious and loving environment for all involved. When blending two families together, it is important to remember that each member brings their own unique experiences, personalities, and expectations to the table.

Communication is key in nurturing a healthy relationship as a blended family. It is essential to create an open and safe space where everyone feels heard and valued. Encourage open dialogue and active listening, and be willing to compromise and find common ground when conflicts arise. Remember that it takes time to build trust and rapport with stepchildren and stepparents, so be patient and give each other the space to adjust to the new family dynamic.

Setting boundaries and establishing clear roles within the blended family is also crucial. Define expectations, rules, and responsibilities early on to avoid confusion and misunderstandings. Encourage mutual respect and appreciation for each other's contributions to the family unit.

Fostering a sense of unity and togetherness within the blended family is essential for building a strong and lasting bond. Create opportunities for quality time together, such as family outings, game nights, or shared meals. Celebrate milestones and achievements as a family, and support each other through life's ups and downs.

By prioritizing communication, setting boundaries, and fostering unity, you can nurture a healthy relationship as a blended family and create a loving and supportive environment for everyone involved. Remember that love, patience, and understanding are the foundation for a successful blended family dynamic.

Chapter 8: Finding Your Soul Mate in a Long-Distance Relationship

Building Trust and Communication in a Long-Distance Relationship

One of the biggest challenges in a long-distance relationship is maintaining trust and communication. When physical distance separates you from your soul mate, it can be easy to feel disconnected and insecure about the strength of your relationship. However, with the right strategies and mindset, you can build a strong foundation of trust and open communication that will help your love thrive despite the miles between you.

First and foremost, it is essential to establish clear and honest communication with your partner. Make an effort to schedule regular video calls, phone calls, and text messages to stay connected and updated on each other's lives. Share your thoughts, feelings, and experiences openly and listen attentively to your partner's as well. Being transparent and vulnerable with each other will help foster a deep sense of trust and intimacy in your relationship.

Additionally, make sure to set expectations and boundaries with your partner regarding communication frequency and availability. Agree on times for regular check-ins and make an effort to prioritize quality time together, even if it's through virtual means. Trust is built on consistency and reliability, so make an effort to honor your commitments to your partner and show them that they can depend on you, regardless of the distance between you.

Lastly, make sure to address any insecurities or doubts that may arise in your long-distance relationship. Be honest with your partner about your fears and concerns, and work together to find solutions that make both of you feel secure and valued. Remember that trust is a two-way street, and it requires effort and commitment from both partners to maintain a healthy and fulfilling relationship, even when you're miles apart. By prioritizing open communication, honesty, and understanding, you can build a strong foundation of trust and love that will help your long-distance relationship flourish.

Planning Visits and Creating Special Moments from Afar

Planning visits and creating special moments from afar is an essential aspect of maintaining a strong connection with your soul mate, especially in a long-distance relationship. While physical distance may separate you, there are numerous ways to stay connected and keep the flame of love burning bright.

One way to plan visits is to set aside specific dates in advance, allowing both partners to make arrangements and look forward to spending quality time together. Whether it's a weekend getaway or an extended vacation, planning visits can create excitement and anticipation, strengthening the bond between soul mates.

Creating special moments from afar is equally important in nurturing your relationship. Technology has made it easier than ever to stay connected, whether through video calls, text messages, or even sending surprise gifts or letters. Taking the time to show your partner that you care and are thinking of them can go a long way in keeping the love alive.

In a long-distance relationship, it's crucial to be creative and find unique ways to make your partner feel loved and appreciated. This could include planning virtual date nights, watching movies together online, or even cooking the same meal and enjoying it together over video call.

Remember, distance is just a test of how far love can travel. By planning visits and creating special moments from afar, you can strengthen your bond with your soul mate and show them that your love knows no boundaries.

Overcoming Challenges and Staying Connected Across the Miles

In the journey to finding your soul mate, challenges are bound to arise, especially when trying to maintain a connection across the miles. Whether you are in a long-distance relationship, have different cultural or religious backgrounds, or are simply struggling to stay connected after a breakup or divorce, it is important to remember that true love knows no boundaries.

One of the key ways to overcome these challenges is through effective communication. Make time to regularly check in with your partner, whether it be through phone calls, video chats, or even handwritten letters. Share your thoughts, feelings, and experiences openly and honestly to ensure that you both feel connected and understood.

Additionally, finding common interests and hobbies to bond over can help bridge the physical distance between you. Consider taking up a new hobby together, such as cooking, painting, or even watching the same TV shows or movies simultaneously. This can create shared experiences and memories that will strengthen your bond and keep you connected.

It is also important to prioritize self-discovery and personal growth in the process of finding your soul mate. Take time to reflect on your own values, beliefs, and goals, and communicate these openly with your partner. Understanding yourself better will not only help you attract the right person into your life but also ensure that you are able to maintain a strong connection despite any challenges that may arise.

Remember, finding your soul mate is a journey that requires patience, resilience, and a willingness to overcome obstacles together. Stay committed to the process, stay connected, and trust that true love will prevail in the end.

Chapter 9: Finding Your Soul Mate Through Self-Discovery and Personal Growth

Reflecting on Your Personal Values and Goals

In the journey to finding your soul mate, it is crucial to take the time to reflect on your personal values and goals. Understanding what is truly important to you will not only help you attract the right partner, but also ensure a fulfilling and lasting relationship.

Take a moment to think about what values are non-negotiable for you in a relationship. Is honesty at the top of your list? How about kindness, loyalty, or ambition? Identifying these core values will guide you in making decisions and setting boundaries in your search for love.

Next, consider your long-term goals and aspirations. Where do you see yourself in five, ten, or twenty years? Do you want to travel the world, start a family, or focus on your career? It is important to find a partner who shares similar goals or is supportive of your ambitions.

When reflecting on your personal values and goals, it is also important to be honest with yourself about any past relationships or experiences that may have shaped your beliefs about love. Take the time to heal from any past heartbreak or trauma before embarking on a new relationship.

By reflecting on your personal values and goals, you will not only attract a partner who aligns with your vision for the future, but also create a strong foundation for a healthy and fulfilling relationship. Remember, true love begins with loving yourself and knowing what you deserve in a partner.

Investing in Self-Care and Personal Development

Investing in self-care and personal development is crucial on the path to finding your soul mate. It is important to take care of yourself physically, mentally, and emotionally in order to attract the right person into your life.

Self-care involves taking the time to prioritize your own well-being. This can include activities such as exercise, meditation, journaling, and spending time with loved ones. By taking care of yourself, you will feel more confident and happy, which will make you more attractive to potential partners.

Personal development is also key in finding your soul mate. This involves reflecting on your past relationships and identifying patterns or behaviors that may be holding you back. By working on yourself and addressing any issues or insecurities, you will be better equipped to enter into a healthy, loving relationship.

Additionally, personal growth can lead to increased self-awareness and a better understanding of what you truly want and need in a partner. By knowing yourself and your values, you will be able to attract someone who aligns with your goals and desires.

Investing in self-care and personal development is a lifelong journey that will not only benefit your romantic relationships but also all aspects of your life. By taking the time to nurture yourself and grow as an individual, you will be on the right path to finding your soul mate and experiencing true love.

Attracting a Soul Mate Who Aligns with Your Authentic Self

Attracting a soul mate who aligns with your authentic self is all about being true to who you are and what you want in a partner. In order to find true love, you must first understand yourself and what you truly desire in a relationship. This means taking the time to reflect on your values, beliefs, and goals in life.

When looking for a soul mate, it is important to focus on finding someone who shares similar interests and values as you. Whether it's through online dating, mutual interests and hobbies, spiritual connections, or compatibility, the key is to find someone who truly understands and appreciates you for who you are.

If you are coming out of a divorce or breakup, it is important to take the time to heal and rediscover yourself before jumping into a new relationship. Finding your soul mate after a heartbreak can be a transformative experience, as it allows you to learn from past mistakes and grow as a person.

For single parents, finding a soul mate can be a bit more challenging, but not impossible. It is important to find someone who not only accepts you as a parent but also embraces your children as part of the package.

Whether you are in a long-distance relationship, same-sex relationship, multicultural or interfaith relationship, or are finding love later in life, the key is to stay true to yourself and your values. By being authentic and honest with yourself and your potential partner, you are more likely to attract a soul mate who aligns with your true self. Remember, true love is worth the wait and the effort it takes to find it.

Chapter 10: Finding Your Soul Mate in a Same-Sex Relationship

Celebrating Love and Connection in Same-Sex Partnerships

In today's world, love knows no boundaries or limitations. Same-sex partnerships are just as beautiful and meaningful as any other form of love, and it is important to celebrate and honor these relationships. Finding your soul mate in a same-sex relationship can be a unique and fulfilling experience, filled with love, connection, and growth.

One of the key aspects of finding your soul mate in a same-sex relationship is understanding and embracing your own identity and authenticity. It is essential to be true to yourself and to be open and honest with your partner about who you are. This level of vulnerability and transparency can deepen the connection between you and your partner, creating a strong foundation for a loving and lasting relationship.

Celebrating love in a same-sex partnership also involves embracing and accepting each other's differences and unique qualities. It is important to respect and honor each other's individuality, while also finding common ground and shared values to build upon. By celebrating the diversity and richness of your relationship, you can create a harmonious and loving partnership.

Finding your soul mate in a same-sex relationship may come with its own set of challenges, but it is important to remember that love knows no boundaries. By staying true to yourself, embracing your partner's uniqueness, and celebrating the love and connection you share, you can create a fulfilling and joyful partnership that transcends any limitations or obstacles. Love is love, and it is worth celebrating in all its forms.

Navigating Challenges and Embracing LGBTQ+ Identity

Finding your soul mate can be a journey filled with challenges, especially for those who identify as LGBTQ+. In a world that is still evolving in terms of acceptance and understanding of diverse sexual orientations and gender identities, it is important to navigate these challenges with strength and resilience.

One of the key aspects of finding your soul mate as a member of the LGBTQ+ community is embracing your identity fully and unapologetically. This means being proud of who you are and not letting societal norms or expectations dictate your search for love. By embracing your LGBTQ+ identity, you are more likely to attract a partner who loves and accepts you for exactly who you are.

When it comes to finding your soul mate in the LGBTQ+ community, it is essential to seek out spaces and communities that are inclusive and supportive. This may include LGBTQ+ events, organizations, or online dating platforms specifically designed for the community. Surrounding yourself with like-minded individuals who understand and celebrate your identity can make the journey to finding your soul mate more fulfilling and empowering.

It is also important to remember that love knows no boundaries, including gender or sexual orientation. Your soul mate may come in a different package than what you initially expected, so keeping an open mind and heart is crucial. By embracing your LGBTQ+ identity and being true to yourself, you are more likely to attract a partner who truly understands and cherishes you for who you are.

Navigating the challenges of finding your soul mate as a member of the LGBTQ+ community can be daunting, but by staying true to yourself and embracing your identity, you are paving the way for a love that is truly authentic and fulfilling.

Finding Support and Community in the LGBTQ+ Dating Scene

In the LGBTQ+ dating scene, finding support and community is crucial in navigating the complexities of relationships and finding your soul mate. Whether you identify as gay, lesbian, bisexual, transgender, queer, or any other sexual orientation or gender identity, it's important to connect with others who understand and support you.

One way to find support in the LGBTQ+ dating scene is to seek out inclusive and affirming spaces. Look for LGBTQ+-friendly bars, clubs, community centers, and events where you can meet like-minded individuals who share your values and interests. These spaces can provide a sense of belonging and acceptance, as well as opportunities to connect with potential partners who are also looking for love.

Another way to find support and community in the LGBTQ+ dating scene is to seek out online resources and forums specifically for LGBTQ+ individuals. Websites, social media groups, and dating apps geared towards the LGBTQ+ community can be valuable tools for making connections, sharing experiences, and finding advice on dating and relationships.

It's also important to surround yourself with supportive friends, family members, and allies who respect and affirm your identity. Having a strong support system can help you feel more confident and secure in yourself, which can make it easier to navigate the ups and downs of dating and relationships.

By finding support and community in the LGBTQ+ dating scene, you can increase your chances of finding your soul mate and building a fulfilling and lasting relationship based on mutual love, respect, and understanding. Remember, you deserve to be loved and supported for who you are, so don't be afraid to seek out the support you need to find true love.

Chapter 11: Finding Your Soul Mate in a Multicultural or Interfaith Relationship

Embracing Diversity and Celebrating Differences in Relationships

In the journey to finding your soul mate, it is important to embrace diversity and celebrate differences in relationships. Every individual is unique, with their own set of beliefs, values, and experiences. When we open ourselves up to different perspectives and ways of thinking, we create a richer and more fulfilling connection with our partner.

One of the keys to finding your soul mate is to be open-minded and accepting of all types of people. Whether you are looking for love through online dating, mutual interests and hobbies, spiritual connections, or any other avenue, it is essential to appreciate the diversity that exists in the world. By doing so, you increase your chances of finding someone who truly complements you and enriches your life.

For those who have experienced heartbreak or are starting over later in life, embracing diversity can be especially beneficial. Being open to different types of relationships and partners can lead to unexpected connections and opportunities for growth. Whether you are a single parent, in a long-distance relationship, or in a same-sex or multicultural partnership, celebrating your differences can strengthen your bond and create a deeper sense of understanding and connection.

Ultimately, finding your soul mate is about finding someone who accepts you for who you are, differences and all. By embracing diversity in relationships and celebrating the unique qualities that each person brings to the table, you increase your chances of finding a truly fulfilling and lasting partnership. So open your heart to the possibilities that exist within the vast tapestry of human experience, and you may just find the love of your life.

Communicating Effectively Across Cultural or Religious Boundaries

In today's interconnected world, it is becoming increasingly common to find love across cultural or religious boundaries. While this can be a beautiful and enriching experience, it also presents its own set of challenges when it comes to effective communication. In order to navigate these differences and build a strong foundation for your relationship, it is important to approach communication with sensitivity, openness, and a willingness to learn from one another.

One key aspect of communicating effectively across cultural or religious boundaries is to approach conversations with an open mind and a genuine curiosity about your partner's beliefs and values. Instead of making assumptions or passing judgment, take the time to ask questions and listen actively to their perspective. This will not only help you to better understand where they are coming from, but also show them that you respect and value their unique background.

Additionally, it is important to be mindful of your own cultural biases and how they may impact your communication with your partner. Be willing to reflect on your own beliefs and be open to challenging them in order to create a more inclusive and harmonious relationship. Remember that communication is a two-way street, and both partners must be willing to put in the effort to bridge any potential gaps that may arise.

By approaching communication with sensitivity, openness, and a willingness to learn, you can build a strong and resilient relationship that transcends cultural or religious boundaries. Embrace the opportunity to learn from one another, celebrate your differences, and grow together as a couple on the path to true love.

Finding Common Ground and Shared Values in a Multicultural Partnership

In a world that is becoming increasingly diverse and interconnected, it is essential to find common ground and shared values in a multicultural partnership. When it comes to finding your soul mate, especially in a multicultural or interfaith relationship, it is important to recognize and appreciate the differences that make each individual unique.

One of the first steps in finding common ground in a multicultural partnership is to have open and honest communication. This means being willing to listen to your partner's perspectives and beliefs, even if they may be different from your own. By actively listening and seeking to understand, you can find areas of overlap and shared values that will strengthen your relationship.

Another key aspect of finding common ground in a multicultural partnership is to celebrate diversity. Rather than seeing differences as barriers, view them as opportunities for growth and learning. Embrace the richness that comes from sharing different cultural backgrounds, traditions, and beliefs.

Finding shared values in a multicultural partnership can also be achieved through mutual respect and compromise. Recognize that there may be times when you will need to make concessions or adjustments to accommodate each other's needs and beliefs. By approaching challenges with empathy and understanding, you can build a strong foundation of trust and respect in your relationship.

Ultimately, finding common ground and shared values in a multicultural partnership requires a willingness to embrace diversity and work towards a harmonious coexistence. By valuing each other's differences and finding ways to connect on a deeper level, you can create a fulfilling and meaningful relationship with your soul mate, regardless of cultural or religious backgrounds.

Chapter 12: Finding Your Soul Mate Later in Life or After Experiencing Heartbreak

Embracing the Journey of Self-Discovery and Growth

In the journey of finding your soul mate, one of the most important aspects to consider is embracing the process of self-discovery and personal growth. This subchapter delves into the idea that in order to attract the right person into your life, you first need to understand and love yourself fully.

Self-discovery is a lifelong journey that involves exploring your values, beliefs, strengths, and weaknesses. By taking the time to reflect on who you are and what you want out of life, you are better equipped to recognize a compatible partner when they come along. This process of self-awareness allows you to set healthy boundaries, communicate effectively, and maintain a strong sense of self in a relationship.

Personal growth is also essential in the quest for true love. As you continue to evolve and improve yourself, you become more attractive to potential partners who are also on a path of growth. This can involve pursuing your passions, learning new skills, and stepping out of your comfort zone. By constantly challenging yourself to become the best version of yourself, you not only enhance your own life but also increase the likelihood of finding a soul mate who shares your values and ambitions.

By embracing the journey of self-discovery and growth, you are not only preparing yourself for a fulfilling and harmonious relationship but also creating a strong foundation for lasting love. Remember, true love begins with loving yourself first.

Letting Go of Past Pain and Opening Your Heart to Love Again

Letting go of past pain is essential in order to open your heart to love again and find your soul mate. Holding onto past hurts and baggage from previous relationships can prevent you from fully embracing a new and potentially fulfilling connection. It is important to take the time to heal and process any pain or trauma you may have experienced in the past before moving forward in your search for true love.

One way to let go of past pain is to practice forgiveness. This doesn't mean you have to forget what happened or excuse the behavior of those who hurt you, but it does mean releasing the negative emotions and resentment that may be holding you back. Forgiveness is a powerful tool that can help you move forward with an open heart and a clear mind.

Another important step in opening your heart to love again is to cultivate self-love and self-care. Treat yourself with kindness and compassion, and prioritize your own well-being. When you love yourself deeply, you are better able to give and receive love from others.

Finally, be open to the possibility of love in all its forms. Your soul mate may come into your life in unexpected ways, through online dating, mutual interests and hobbies, spiritual connections, or personal growth and self-discovery. Stay open to the journey and trust that the universe will bring the right person into your life at the right time.

By letting go of past pain and opening your heart to love again, you are creating space for true love to enter your life. Trust in the process and believe that you are deserving of a deep and meaningful connection with your soul mate.

Finding Hope and Renewed Purpose in Finding Your Soul Mate later in Life

Finding hope and renewed purpose in finding your soul mate later in life can be a truly transformative experience. Many people believe that the opportunity for true love diminishes as we age, but this is simply not true. In fact, finding your soul mate later in life can bring a sense of fulfillment and joy that may not have been possible earlier on in your journey.

One of the key aspects of finding your soul mate later in life is the wisdom and experience that you bring to the table. You have likely been through relationships that have taught you valuable lessons about what you truly want and need in a partner. This self-discovery can lead to a deeper understanding of yourself and what you are looking for in a soul mate.

Additionally, finding your soul mate later in life can bring a renewed sense of purpose and hope. After experiencing heartbreak or disappointment in the past, finding true love can feel like a second chance at happiness. This can be incredibly empowering and can help you approach your relationship with a newfound sense of gratitude and appreciation.

Whether you are finding your soul mate through online dating, mutual interests and hobbies, spiritual connections, or any other means, remember that love knows no age limit. Embrace the journey of finding your soul mate later in life and allow yourself to be open to the possibilities that await you. Trust that the universe has a plan for you and that true love is always within reach, no matter where you are in your life's journey.

Milton Keynes UK
Ingram Content Group UK Ltd.
UKHW020314200324
439698UK00024B/666